T0137613

I AM THE
SOLDIER

ANN MARIE

authorHOUSE®

AuthorHouse™
1663 Liberty Drive
Bloomington, IN 47403
www.authorhouse.com
Phone: 1 (800) 839-8640

Published by AuthorHouse 08/04/2016

ISBN: 978-1-5246-1684-7 (sc)
ISBN: 978-1-5246-1683-0 (e)

Print information available on the last page.

Any people depicted in stock imagery provided by Thinkstock are models, and such images are being used for illustrative purposes only. Certain stock imagery © Thinkstock.

This book is printed on acid-free paper.

Because of the dynamic nature of the Internet, any web addresses or links contained in this book may have changed since publication and may no longer be valid. The views expressed in this work are solely those of the author and do not necessarily reflect the views of the publisher, and the publisher hereby disclaims any responsibility for them.

Contents

Prologue

My Book "I AM THE SOLDIER" is a series of short stories written in poetry form. These poems reflect the basic emotions experienced by Military families when loved ones are called to serve. Each poem will take the reader on this emotional journey.

An earlier conversation with a family member who had a loved one away on active Military duty gave me the idea to write this book. The emotions that resonated during the conversation were emotions of fear; longing, loneliness and missing that are captured in this book.

This book is to all families whose lives have been touched by change and by absence. It is to those whose loved ones are away on active duty; to those whose loved ones are preparing to begin their tour and to those whose loved ones have returned home.

My Soldier,

Although we miss you, we fully support the stand you have taken to protect us.

So do not fear

Do not despair

Know we will always be here

My Husband the Soldier

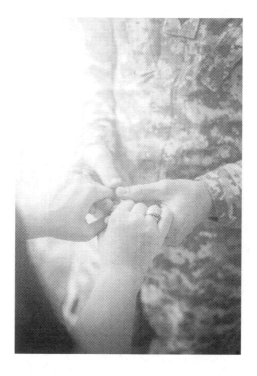

The order came to protect and serve
He packed his bags without a word
As he boarded the plane he smiled and waved
I wondered if I'd ever see him again.

He stepped inside and he was gone
How will I ever go on?
The pain inside is so very real
It's hard to describe the way I feel.

I glanced up as the plane took off
All around me there was not a sound
The silence did not the engine drown
There was not a dried eye as I glanced around.

I took one step and then another
I walked to the car as if in a daze
The gently tug on my arms
Made me stopped and looked into my children's gaze.

I looked into the eyes of my son and daughter
I could tell how much they were missing their father
What can I tell them I thought with fear?
What would bring the most comfort to their ears?

They must be hurting as much as I am
How can I help them understand
Tell me that I can do this
Please tell me that I can.

With throat constricting I gently said
"It's going to be all right
We'll say a prayer for Daddy tonight."
"We'll pray and pray until he comes home
And when our prayers reach him, he'll know he's
    not alone."

I knelt down and held my children tight
"Sweet darlings, it's going to be alright"
There was a gently peace felt by all
And at that moment I knew my children understood
That their daddy went to protect us all
So that against tyranny we would not fall.

As I drove away
I took one last glance upward high
The plane was now a mere dot in the sky
Do I dare ask the question, "Why?"

I don't suppose I should
My husband was called to serve
A long time ago
He had made an oath that he would.

Now that time had come for him to keep that promise
The time had come for me to be brave
The time had come for me to step up to the plate
And not show resentment or feel any hate.

I knew I had to be strong
I knew I could not breakdown
I knew I could not show despair
But deep down inside I was trembling with fear.

"Mommy"
The tiny voice came from the back seat of the car
It sounded so distant like from afar
"Yes my darling" I answered softly
All the time trying to choke back the tears
"When's my daddy coming home?"
That question made me aged in years.

Oh I was not prepared for that!
What do I do?
What do I say?
Oh I wish this would all go away!

I pinched myself once, then twice
Almost to the point to make me scream
Hoping that by some miracle
I would wake up from what seemed like a terrible
    dream.

But I was awake! Wide-awake!
And I had just sent my husband off to war
When is he coming home?
I did not know
This was not an easy answer by far.

I had to push aside my fear
And reach deep inside my heart
Pulled from my inner self and
Found the strength that I needed there.

"My darlings", was that my voice?
It sounded so strong.
"That can't be me." I thought,
It was like I had prepared for this moment all along.

"Daddy will come home when he has done his duty,
However long it takes
Through our prayers he will know that we are here
    waiting for him
Despite our heartaches."

"He will feel it in his heart
He will feel it cause we're apart
He will sense our love for him
He will know that we care
He will see our smiling faces
And know that we will be here."

My son smiled and nodded his head
"I am so proud of my daddy", he said
At that moment my heart raced with joy
I felt an inner peace
As I smiled at my sweet baby boy.

I looked up for one last glance of the plane
And wandered in my heart
Dear Husband,
Will I ever see him again?

My Dad the Soldier

My daddy is going away today
For me it's a very sad, sad day
He hugged me as he said goodbye
And whispered softly that I should not cry.

He hugged my mommy and sister too
He kissed their cheeks and said
"I'm going to miss you."

I watched as my daddy walked away and burst into tears
I'm going to miss him so much
He will be gone for almost two years
Although I knew in my heart that he could not stay
But he was going so far away.

My mommy came and took my hand
Her eyes pleading for me to understand
"I'm going to miss him mommy" I said with sad eyes
"I know my darling" my mommy replied
As we held each other and just cried.

My sister came over and we stood, us three
"Mommy," she said.
"I hope my daddy comes back to me."

I looked at my sister and she appeared so calm
But her eyes were filled with tears
She turned and looked at me
It was right at that moment I knew
She was missing daddy as much as I do.

I turned and looked as my daddy boarded the plane
I stared at his back and wondered if I'd ever see him
    again
At the top of the steps my dad smiled and waved
I stood very still at attention trying very hard to be brave.

Then he stepped inside and he was gone
I must have stood there for however long
The gently arm on my shoulder
Made me look up at the face of my mother
Who not daring to say a word
The silence around me was all that I heard.

The plane taxied on the runway for a little while
It's going around in circles I thought with a smile
As it gained some speed my heart seemed to stop
I stared and stared until my eyes felt like they
    would pop.

My eyes and my heart followed the plane as it flew
    into the air
Hoping against hope that it would not disappear
My daddy is on that plane
My daddy is going away to some far off place
Oh! I wish that he could stay with us
But a long time ago he had taken an oath
And so to protect his country was a must.

I felt it wet on my cheek
It was as if I had sprung a leak
I was crying so hard I could not stop
First one drop, then two drops
…Then three
Oh! I wish my daddy would come back to me.

I looked at my sister and saw she was crying too
My mommy seemed so helpless, not knowing what
    to do
"Give me strength," I heard her say
Help us to get through this sad, sad day

We held each other and stood for a while
Then, "come my darlings," my mother said with a
    smile
She took our hands and we walked slowly to the car
It was the longest walk I had ever taken by far

I glanced back at the plane now a mere dot in the sky
Is this all worth it
Might I ask the question – "Why?"

My Son the Soldier

The smiling face stared at me
From a picture on the mantle
Next to it was a single candle
There was something so special
About that smile I thought
It was the smile of my son
Whom into the world I brought

I remembered it as if it was yesterday
Winter was gone and spring had come out to play
You took us by surprise you know
You came earlier than we expected
Before the flowers had time to blossom and grow

From the moment I laid eyes on you
Somehow I knew you would be great
I knew that you would become the man
I would grow to appreciate

When you were young I could tell
By the way you would stare well
Off into the distance
I could see it in you eyes
That you wanted to do more with your life
And hoped that there would be no resistance

You decided that you wanted to be a soldier
A long time ago
You wanted to follow in the footsteps
Of the brave men and women who had gone before
Since the beginning of creation
Who fought and gave their lives
To protect and build this great nation

I felt your passion to commit to serve
I could hear it in your voice when you told me
You wanted to enlist, I said not a word
I told myself there was a greater purpose
For you in this world
And at the time I was not surprised
For I could see it in your eyes

And now we are standing here
With you leaving and me bidding you farewell
My emotions are running so deep right now
My heart is full and I am crying inside
But my face is brave so it's hard to tell

You are going off to war
You are going to a far off place
I know I have to let you go
I am scared but yet so proud
I planted a seed and I lived to see it grow
So farewell my son and take care
Know you will be in my every thought and prayer

In the mean time
I will wait for your safe return
I will light the candle
Every day by your picture on the mantle
And watch it slowly burn

I am so proud to call you my son
You are and forever my inspiration
With your decision to fight for what's right
For me the battle is already won

My Wife the Soldier

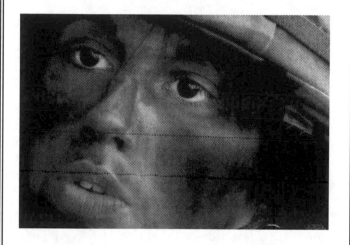

Mother

Daughter

Sister

Aunt

Niece

Cousin

Sister-in-law

Friend

My wife and my life

As I watched you pack your bags to leave
I struggled very hard to breathe
To know you were going away
When in my heart I wanted you to stay

I kept thinking to myself
Will I ever see her again?
Then you looked up at me and smiled
With a reassurance in your eyes
That everything will be all right

There were no words that followed that look
But it spoke volumes
More than any words could say
That was ever written in a book

When you reached for my hand and gently squeezed
I knew you wanted me to understand and believe
That this was not goodbye; you had a duty to fulfill
A long time ago you took an oath that you will

Fight to defend the future of this great country
To guarantee a future for us from tyranny
To make a world so that our children can run free
A world where they can lie and dream under any tree

You finished packing and it was time
There were so many mixed feelings
Running through my mind
I was trying very hard not to think about the what
    ifs
Or how I was going to get through this!

I tried to put myself in a happy place
To hold on to the memories that we have already
    made
To revel in the joy that we will make many more
In the future when you walked back through the
    door

This is my hope, and I know it is yours too
But for now, I know you must go and do

I am so proud of you my heart
I have loved you right from the start
And I want you to know
It will be hard for me let you go

I am trying my best to be brave
I am trying very hard not to be selfish
I know it must be very hard for you to leave
Oh! I wish! I wish! I wish!

Rest assured while you are gone
I promise to hold down the fort at home
I will take care of our kids
I will look in on your family
I will be all that I can be
I will be waiting here
For your safe return to me

I love you now and forever
You are my joy and my inspiration
You are my wife
You are my life
And I will leave you, never!

I am the soldier

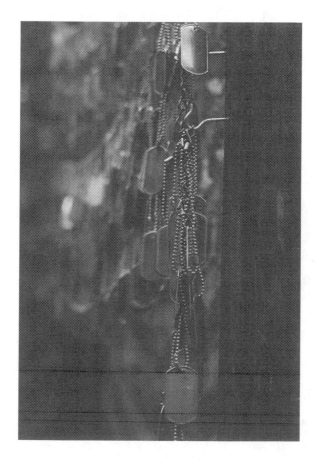

You might find this hard to believe
But being a soldier have always been my dream
So I want you to know when the order came
I was very happy to see my name

To know that I was going to make a difference in
Someone else's life
To let them know there was hope amidst all the
War and strife

So when you look at my broken body
Even though it's missing an arm or a leg or both
And I should be standing upright as any able
Bodied soldier should
Know that if I could do it all over again I would

The price I had to pay is very minimal to what I
Saw and lived each day
The battle was long and hard
And it was not an easy feat
Sometimes I walked for miles and miles
Without stopping to sleep or eat

For although my feet would hurt and my eyes
Full of sand
I knew I had to carry on for there was a greater
Purpose at hand

I guess I was luckier than most
Because I lost my friends and fellow soldiers
When they invaded our post

I need for you to understand
We do live in a very blessed land
We take for granted the very air we breathe
While others suffer and are in dire need

The oath that I took when I became a soldier
Was to protect and serve the human race
My service was not limited only to those in the
United States

You see we are human first and foremost
And we are all here for a greater purpose
I know the thought of going to war makes
Everybody nervous

But I want you to know
Despite all the turmoil focused was never lost
We knew we had a mission to complete
And we did so at every cost

So I am hoping that my family
Would understand
Although my body is broken
I am not a broken man

I feel comforted in the fact that
I fought the good fight
I did all that was asked of me
This was what I signed up for
To be all that I can be

Remember when I took the oath
I agreed to the stipulation
That I would stand up to tyranny
Both at home and in other nations

I know you are sad
And might be very mad
But I know that because of me
Other nations will eventually be free

To my Soldier

The feelings that followed on the day you left
Are ones I cannot and will not soon forget
I watched your plane taxied and flew away
And wondered how I was going to get through that
      sad day

It was shear will power that moved my feet
My steps were in sync to my heartbeat
In the car I wanted to breakdown and cry
For it was such a sad occasion that no one could deny

When we got home I kept hoping,
Listening, praying for the phone to ring
Hoping it would be you on the other end of the line
Telling me how you hated to leave me behind

Telling me the plans had changed
That there was no need to be engaged
And I would no longer be alone
Because you were on your way back home

But when the phone did not ring
Panic started to set in
It was then I realized this was real
That you had been sent out into the field

I try to stay busy throughout each day
But the nights are so much worse
It's very hard to keep the butterflies away
And concentrate on things to keep me immersed

I always knew this time would come
But for me it came too soon
I miss you, my love, my own
It's so hard and sad to be alone

To be separated from you is breaking my heart
Oh! I can't stand that we are apart
I need you to be safe and come back to me
But I know right now, you have to be all you can be

I want you to know the kids are ok
We are learning to take it slowly day by day
I try my best to keep you alive in their eyes
By sticking to our routine and not breakdown and
    cry

Our family and friends have truly been supportive
I know that they really care and have no ulterior
motives
It has been truly nice to know they are standing by
To lend a helping hand or volunteer a shoulder on
which to cry

Enough about me I do not mean to sound selfish
But you coming home is my deepest wish
I pray everyday for your safe return home
I pray for you to know you are not alone

Even though you are a world away
I hope it gives you strength to know that I am here
to stay
I want you to know that we are in this together
Take care my brave and courageous Soldier
Know that I love you now, always and forever

From my Soldier

I was really happy to receive your letter
Hearing from you made me feel so much better
I hoped and prayed you were doing okay
With me gone and being so far away

I believe next week sometime is when I can call
They say we can even face time, if I recall
The anticipation of seeing you is wearing me thin
I miss you so much; I do not know where to begin

Thanks for the care package I loved it
It had all the favorite items from my wish list
My fellow soldiers tease me that I'm spoiled
I tease them right back, but do so with a smile

You have always been there and taken care of me
You are in deed my better half; I know my mom
    would agree
She thinks so highly of you, in fact, both my parents do
I knew my dreams had come true the day I married you

I cannot wait to see you and hear your voice
It will be like a breath of fresh air amidst all the noise
Right now we have to be cautious, careful if you will
We have had a few surprises that brought everything
    to a standstill

The days have been long and hard
We have to constantly be on our guard
For anything strange or suspicious
For anything that could fatally harm us

Ann Marie

It is very hard to smile or talk to a stranger
For in doing so could put us in imminent danger
Our minds have to always be in a defensive mode
We have to one hundred percent live by the safety code

Out here there are a lot of brave men and women
Like me, they are willing to fight to the end
Like me, they have left families and friends at home
Whom we hope to see again when our tour here is
    done

In civilian clothes we stand alone as strangers
But in our uniforms we come together as brothers
Whether we are in the Marines, Navy, Air force or
    Army
We all made the sacred oath to serve and protect
    our country

As we struggle to put our best foot forward day by
    day
We know that we would not have it any other way
We have a duty to perform and we do so in good
    spirit
We are here to protect and serve we are not here to
    quit

So take care my darling and be brave for me
You are forever imprinted in my memory
You are my ray of sunshine on those dark days
I love you now, forever and always

The WALK

Who knows where life's journey will take us
Will it be somewhere we want to go?
How far will we be willing to travel thus
Without direction in hand or a compass

For we know not the day nor the time
When we have reached the end of the line
Will we go peacefully?
Without a worry of what we are leaving behind?

Let us hope when that time comes
When we hear the beat of the silent drum
When we have to take The Walk onward
We will do so willing and not be a coward

While looking forward to our new journey ahead
of us
With the peace of mind and heart for in God We
Trust
That we have completed our journey here on earth
And left a legacy behind that will be of much worth

About the Author

The Author is a Jamaican born U.S. citizen. She has called America home for the past twenty two years. She is married and has two children. Growing up she always had a passion for reading, which later transformed into a love for writing. She wanted to tell stories but to tell them in a way that would captivate and inspire her readers, pulling them into her world and allowing them to see through her eyes the unspoken emotions of individuals when they are faced with trying situations. Her book 'I Am The Soldier' captures these emotions and presents a connection with her readers' from start to finish.

Printed in the United States
By Bookmasters